I0103727

Jane Bancroft

A study of the Parliament of Paris and the other parliaments of France

Jane Bancroft

A study of the Parliament of Paris and the other parliaments of France

ISBN/EAN: 9783337151010

Printed in Europe, USA, Canada, Australia, Japan

Cover: Foto ©Suzi / pixelio.de

More available books at **www.hansebooks.com**

A STUDY

OF THE

PARLIAMENT OF PARIS,

AND THE OTHER

PARLIAMENTS OF FRANCE.

A THESIS

PRESENTED TO THE FACULTY OF THE COLLEGE OF LIBERAL ARTS

OF THE SYRACUSE UNIVERSITY,

FOR THE ATTAINMENT OF THE DEGREE OF

DOCTOR OF PHILOSOPHY,

- BY -

JANE M. BANCROFT,

OF

THE NORTHWESTERN UNIVERSITY, EVANSTON, ILL.

Introductory Note.

———

The subject of the Parliaments of France, so far as I am aware, is treated by no one English author. While frequent allusions are made to the Parliaments in all histories of France, somewhat diligent search has failed to find in any English work an adequate explanation of their origin, their organization, and their political history. The collection of materials for even so short a thesis, has therefore been attended with considerable difficulty. The translations of the authorities quoted in the notes, are, in all cases, those of the writer.

I desire to acknowledge obligation for valuable assistance rendered in prosecuting my studies, to Miss Florence Cushing, of Boston; to Mr. John Savary, Assistant Librarian of the Library of Congress; to Mr. Frederick Saunders, Superintendent of the Astor Library, and to Dr. W. F. Poole, of the Library of Chicago.

JANE M. BANCROFT.

Woman's College of the
Northwestern University, Evanston, Ill.
June 11, 1884.

4

information and advice concerning matters of state; a council which filled the function of both a political and feudal assembly.[1]

A brief résumé of the reasons for the several theories will be given.

I. If it could be proved that France had a judicial system extending backward in an unbroken chain, so that the Parliaments could be connected with the Champs de Mai, under the Carlovingian rulers, and the Champs de Mars, under the Merovingian fainéants, then the right of the people to a voice in government would receive historical corroboration, and the Parliaments would be its still existing monuments. In the troubled state of France preceding the Great Revolution industrious researches were made to sustain this theory, and its best presentation is found in the famous Encyclopædia edited by Diderot, and d' Alembert.[2] The assemblies of the nation, to which historians have applied the name parlemens généraux were not of royal institution, but were brought in by the Franks. Under the first race they were called "Mallum,"[3] from the Teutonic mallen to talk; under the second race, they were known as Mallum, placitum generale, consilium, or colloquium; under the third race, curia regis, judicium Francorum, and subsequently parlement. At first all freemen were admitted to these assemblies; as the nation became greater, each canton had its own assembly, and only those who held rank or position in the state were admitted. These general assemblies formed the public council of the kings. Furthermore, the kings of the first and second races had their special council or court, and toward

---

[1] Beugnot, Comte de. Documents inédits sur l' Hist. de France. Les Olim, vol. 1, préface. p. 29.

[2] Encyclopédie Méthodique, Jurisprudence, tome vi, Paris 1786.

[3] Gibert, Recherch, histr, sur les Cours de Justice, tome 30, p. 592. Le mot Parlementum avait la même signification que celui de mallum, qui dans l'ancienne langue, voulait dire, conférence pour parler.

the close of the second race, the parlemens généraux were chosen from members of the king's court. The reunion of the public and special council was consummated during the first three centuries of the third race. The assembly of the king's court was never identical with the old assemblies of the nation. The latter were not of royal creation, and those who formed part of it enjoyed this right, by virtue of being freemen. The king's court of council was of his own creation. Its existence and powers depended upon his will. Thus, the editors of the Encyclopædia regard the Parliament as a transformed institution, arising from the general assemblies of the first race, the council and general assemblies of the second, and the council of the third race, being in each case the institution, which, with the king, considered the highest interests of the kingdom and pronounced ultimate sentence of justice.

II. The claims of four several kings of the third race to be considered as the founder of Parliament, need to be examined.

a. [1]M. de La Roche-Flavin, a celebrated parliamentarian, holds that the Parliament of Paris had its origin in the Assembly ordered by Pepin-le-Bref. Having resolved to go in person to Italy to aid the Pope against the Lombards, and having invited the majority of the princes and great lords to accompany him, he ordered a council or Parliament, "composed of certain men of fame and experience," in his name and by his authority to consider important matters, and to render sovereign justice in his absence. De La Roche-Flavin thinks that this body continued an irregular existence, meeting when the king found most convenient, and as public matters demanded.

b. Others accord this honor to Philippe Auguste. His father, Louis-le-Gros, influenced by the popular legends of Arthur

---

[1] Bernard de La Roche-Flavin, Les Parlements de France, treize livres. Paris, 1621.

and his knights,[1] had created twelve peers, six secular, six ecclesiastical. Philippe Auguste formed from these twelve great lords what he called the Court of Peers,[2] and their first case was the trial of John of England for his failure in duty to his feudal suzerain. When the English king refused to heed the summons of herald and bailiff unless he could be assured of a safe return, the Court of Peers condemned him by default, and all of his possessions in France were forfeited to the crown. This exercise of authority greatly struck the minds of the time, and increased respect was accorded the shrewd lawyer-king who had skillfully dictated the sentence to the court; but there are no other instances in which this body of peers in separate judicial existence exercised authority. After this one memorable act of policy rather than justice, they re-entered the ordinary court of the king, which continued to pronounce judgment as formerly.

c. Under St. Louis the enlargement of the Royal Domain greatly extended the administration of justice, and this king introduced many valuable judicial reforms. But the forms of decrees do not vary from those that had been issued by the three preceding kings, and while St. Louis seems to have more definitely provided for the judicial functions exercised by his court, a comparison of historical proof does not warrant the conclusion that he is the creator of this court.[3]

d. Philippe le Bel, by an edict of May 23, 1302,[4] made the Parliament sedentary at Paris. From this fact, careless historians have ascribed to him the creation of the parliament,

---

[1] Sir James Stephen, Lect. on French Hist.; Lect. viii, p. 206.

[2] Martin, H., Hist. de France, tome iii, p. 582.

[3] Martin, H., Hist. de France, tome iii, p. 294. So good an authority as Martin seems to favor this theory, "Un nom nouveau désigna cette institution nouvelle, le nom de parlement, qui jusqu'alors s'etait appliqué vaguement à toute espéce de conférence.

[4] Maurice Block, Dictionnaire de le Politique, 1880, vol. ii, p. 503.

but this edict merely sanctioned the custom which the Parliament
for half a century had had of holding its sessions at Paris,
and extended its powers to some other judicial bodies.[1]

III. The present century has produced a number of valuable works on the Parliament of Paris and the Parliaments of
France, and a more scientific method of dealing with historical
questions has given better results. What has been called the
third theory, i. e., that the Parliament of Paris was an outgrowth
of the king's council as devoted to judicial functions, has received
the sanction of the late historians, and as Fayard says "rests upon
numerous and irrefragible documents."[2] Before stating the
reasons for the acceptance of the third theory, it will be necessary
to make a digression and study the judicial system in France
during the third race to the opening of the 13th century.

Under feudalism, justice belonged to the lord in his domain.
The whole of France was divided into fiefs or chartered
municipalities. In every fief the lord exercised
hereditary jurisdiction. According to the language of
those times the justice of each Seigneur was either Haute,
Moyenne or Basse, according to the extent of the damages and
the nature of the penalties his court was competent to award.
Every enfranchised municipality also possessed a local tribunal,
which administered justice Haute, Moyenne or Basse according
to the terms of its charter, or its hereditary privileges. The
Seigneur himself presided in the Seignorial Court, and his vassals
attended him as judicial assessors. They were called peers, or
the equals of those who were to come before them for judgment,
for the principle that no man could be tried save by his peers was
as ancient and as fully recognized in France as in England.[3]

Judicial Institutions.

---

[1] Martin H., Hist. de France, tome iv, p. 446.
[2] Aperçu historique sur le Parlement de Paris, E. Fayard, 1876, vol. i, p. 60.
[3] Picot, Georges, Histoire des Etats-Généraux, vol. i, p. 15; Paris, 1872.

"The feudal court, the union of vassals around the suzerain, was the sole vestige that remained of the great principle of deliberation in common, during the course of the tenth century." The king himself was the Seigneur of the greatest fief of the realm, the Royal Domain. The feudal court of the Royal Domain was the exact counterpart of the other feudal or seignorial courts, except that it was presided over, not by the king in person, but the Seneschal, his representative.

But there were questions that did not fall within the range of feudal law and jurisprudence, therefore, in the provinces directly possessed by the descendants of Hugh Capet, Prévôts. judicial powers were intrusted to Prévôts, who at the same time had care of the administration of the domain. This officer became the judge in all non-feudal cases and was charged with punishing slight misdemeanors. He was obliged to hold assizes in all the principal towns. The Prévôts were chosen from the simple bourgeois and were under the immediate authority of the Seneschal. As the Royal Domain enlarged, the courts of the Prévôts and the Seneschal became inadequate for the added duties.

Philip Augustus reverted to one of the Carlovingian institutions. Charlemagne had sent officers called " missi dominici" Missi Dominici. through every province of the empire to redress all grievances and annually to report to him the wants and conditions of all classes of his people.[1] So Philip Augustus appointed migratory commissioners to perform circuits throughout his domain, to listen to all complaints and to transmit them to the king. They were called Baillis, their offices soon became permanent, and their circuits well defined judicial districts and were called Bailliages. The Baillis seem to have been inter-

[1] Martin, II., tome iv, p 298. Capitularies, 810. "The missi dominici were sent by the Emperor with very extended powers, to accomplish, to inspect and even to revise the work of justice."

mediate between the Prévôts and Seneschal, for as soon as the custom of appeals (unknown to feudalism) was established, they exercised the right of judging appeals from the Prévôts. As agents of the royal power, to them belonged the duty of causing the nobles to execute the ordinances of the king.

The seigneurs, "hauts justiciars" in their own domains, were jealous of these judicial encroachments, and were not long in imitating the example of the king, by appointing in their fiefs Seneschals, Prévôts and Baillis. The resemblance was imperfect as the seignorial Baillis could take cognisance of no question beyond his lord's fief, while the King's Baillis could, at need, indict the Seigneur himself. Still, it produced this fortunate result, that as one great fief after another was absorbed into the Royal Domain, the legal machinery adjusted itself to the change of masters without a jar. Thus the absorption of fiefs, by which France became one kingdom, was greatly facilitated. At the summit of this irregular hierarchy was the king's council, charged at all times with the political affairs of the kingdom, and now recognized as the seat of the final judicial authority, the point whence all appeals ended.

When the Crusaders returned from Constantinople, they brought with them great reverence for Roman law. Many of the traditions of the Code of Theodosious had lingered in
Roman law
. the judicial life of France, especially in the southern provinces,[1] but when the Pandects of Justinian were found at Amalfi in 1137 a genuine revival of the study of Roman law took place in the Universities of France and Italy. Bologna became celebrated for her jurisconsults, and the University of Paris numbered thousands of students. [2] Compilations of the customs and local laws of the different provinces had previously

---

[1] Vicomte de Bastard d' Estang, Les Parlements de France, vol. 1, p.43.
[2] The Pope understood the danger to the Church and in 1274 forbade the study of Roman law at Paris. Martin, H., tome iv, p. 291.
2

been made, and these were now annotated in the spirit of the
Digests of Justinian. A certain design is apparent in the tone
of these comments, i. e., the elevation of kingly power, and
the abasement of the great nobles.¹ St. Louis ordered a general
code to be arranged, and the body of feudal law, illustrated by
observations and explanations from the Roman law, was put forth
in the form known as the Etablissements of St. Louis.² This
code was intended for the royal courts in the personal domain of
the king, but it gradually penetrated into the seignorial courts.
Up to this time the seigneur presiding over his assizes had
judged the cases that came before him with prompt and trenchant
decision. When issues were involved that were not clearly
defined by customary usage, recourse was had to various ordeals.
"The defendant must plunge his arm into boiling water, and
withdraw it uninjured; or must walk over a pan of coals, and yet
not be burned; or with his arms tied be thrown into water, and
then sink, which was not so difficult; in this way the suitor was
referred to the judgment of God, and the judge saved all per-
plexing anxiety.

Were the suitor yet unsatisfied, a singular custom of feudal
law gave him a final resource. He could declare the judgment
false, on condition of fighting a duel with each one of
the judges who had declared against him.⁴ St. Louis,
though a deeply religious, was not a superstitious man, and he
clearly perceived that this judicial combat was but to abandon
the weak and old to the strong and vigorous. In 1260, he
issued an ordinance forbidding the duel in all the jurisdictions of

¹ Les Coustumes du Beauvoisis, de Beaumanoir.
Le Conseil à mon ami, par Fontaine. "Le livre de Fontaine, Le
Conseil à mon ami, est le résultat de l' ancienne jurisprudence française
et de la loi romaine," Montesquieu, Esprit des Lois, liv. xxviii, chap. 38.
² Fayard, E. Aperçu historique sur le Parlement de Paris, vol. i, p. 61.
³ Lacombe, Pet. Hist. du Peuple Français, p. 41.
⁴ Picot, Hist. des Etats-Gen. Organisations judiciaries, vol. i, p. 106.

his own domain, replacing it, in cases of appeal by a new examination of the matter before the king's court.[1] This ordinance had been issued only for his own courts, but, it will be remembered, the Baillis had circuits throughout entire France, and in this way were brought into relations with the Seigneurs. When complaints were made of the failure of any lord to do his duty, the Baillis, instead of permitting the judicial combat, insisted that the king's ordinance of 1260 was the rule of judgment, and required the accused to bring proofs and present arguments. This was virtually receiving appeals. If the Baillis were unable to decide the matter, they brought it to the king's knowledge in the presence of his council. The courts of the seigneurs soon became mere tribunals for unimportant cases.

The lawyers, who had been studying the Pandects, were finding other effective ways to increase royal authority. The whole feudal law rested upon the possession of land, as the feudal maxim proves "sans terre sans seigneur;" the Roman law rested upon the relation of subject to king, and king to God; the abstract right of the sovereign was independent of all ownership.[2]

Roman law favorable to kingship.

In the study of this law and the promulgation of its theories, kingly authority found justification for all the power it chose to exert. The legists observing that every imperial command had been binding throughout the Roman Empire, maintained that every sentence pronounced by the King's Courts should be binding throughout France. This was not only to make the laws of the king universal, but to make him a legislator; a power which, in the hands of St. Louis, might not be disastrous

[1] Martin H. Hist. de France, tome iv, p. 301.

[2] Fayard, Aperçu Hist. sur le Parl de Paris, vol. i, p. 87.
Sir Henry Maine, Early Hist. of Institutions, chapter i.
Freeman, E. A., Comparative Politics, Lect. iv, The King.

to a people, but which in the long results of many reigns was to conduct to the absolutism of Louis XIV.

Again, as feudal ties weakened, it became a legal maxim that a suitor might "declare his domicile," that is he could decide for himself whether he would be judged as a vassal of the lord in whose domains he lived, or as a vassal of the great suzerain, the king. In the latter case, he was tried in the King's Courts. There were many reasons why a vassal should prefer the impartial judgment of the latter tribunal, to the partisan decision of the seigneur whose interests were at stake. It is a cause of wonder that the imperious barons acquiesced so quietly in these usurpations, but the code of St. Louis was issued near the close of his reign, when the nobles were absorbed in preparations for the great Crusade. Then, although proud and haughty, these men were ignorant and little disposed to see the drift of subtle questions of law, while St. Louis had the art of interesting them in the acceptance of these reforms, by assuring to them all fines for misdemeanors committed on their lands; he harmonized their prejudices while reforming institutions. Then, too, the barons viewed St. Louis with love, almost with veneration; they regarded him as wise and good, and they saw that his measures were of a generous and national character. Although of so intense a religious nature, he vigorously repelled papal encroachment, and laid the foundation of the liberties of the Gallican Church by the Pragmatic Sanction.[1] Yet this very measure was issued by him as a law resting on his kingly authority, not on the people's sanction.

At his accession in 1226, there had already existed for some time a division or section of the Royal Council known as the

Chambre aux Plaids. Chambre aux Plaids, which considered all appeals and judicial questions. Under St. Louis, this section

---

[1] Martin, H., Hist. de France, tome iv, p. 310.

became sedentary, and formed the Parliament. Twenty-four members of his royal council were assigned to it, and to aid them he appointed twenty legists, or men versed in the study of the law. These humble clerks had previously found entrance there.[1] "So long as disputed questions of law confined themselves to the rights in fishing and hunting, or the payment of feudal dues, the active and warlike barons found no trouble in legislation, but now law was becoming a science. The once satisfactory ordeals were superseded by more delicate tests. The exact truth must be found as to the language and acts alleged, admitted, or denied; the points of law involved, determined; the balance of conflicting testimony weighed.[3] This was an unwelcome change to the untutored nobles. Small stools were brought in and placed below the stately benches of the judges. Here sat the legists, base-born roturiers in mean black gowns, but trained at Bologna or Paris in the study of the Roman law, and curiously gifted with the art of untangling the web of legal difficulties, and deducing the just conclusion. The lords, knights, and prelates' at first listened patiently to long-drawn discussions about rules of law they could not comprehend, and Latin quotations they did not understand; but the hunting-fray and the tournament were calling them away, and the weary hours became intolerable. Especially thankless did the task appear, when at the close of every session it was found that the humble clerks in the black gowns and caps, while affecting to suggest the decisions of the court, had really dictated the answers of the illiterate barons. From this moment the great vassals of

---

[1] Beugnot, Comte de. Essai sur l'organ judic. p. 3.   On ne peut déterminer avec précision à quelle époque commença cette entrée des légistes; mais il est certain que plusieurs des juges sont "qualifiés clericos,, dans un arrêt rendu en 1222.

[3] Desmaze, C. Le Parlement de Paris, avec une Notice sur les autres Parlements de France, Paris, 1859. Chap. i, p. 9.

[8] Martin, Hist. de France, tome iv, p. 310.

the crown began to abandon judicial functions to the men of law, but as peers they always remained members of Parliament, and appeared there when suits concerning their equals were involved, or in grave cases when their opinion was necessary. For all ordinary cases, the *conseiller clercs*, as they were called, were left to themselves. They exchanged the low "marche-pieds" for the vacant benches, and soon obtained titles recognizing the real importance of their office. [1]"They constituted a formidable judicial aristocracy opposite the feudal and sacerdotal aristocracies, and more out of ambition than gratitude they confounded law with the throne, and employed the royal scepter to break the swords of the noblemen and the crosier of the prelates."[2]

Philippe le Bel thought of appropriating the organization of Parliament to the reforms he purposed to accomplish. By an ordinance of May 23, 1302, he ordained "for the convenience of his subjects and the expedition of affairs, there should be held every year two sittings of the Parliament of Paris." We have now before us an outline of the judicial institutions extending to the time when historical truth becomes easy to verify, and the question of the origin of the Parliament of Paris is again reached.

It cannot be doubted that the tradition of old Roman law and the force of local customs lingered on through all changes,[3]

Reasons in Favor of the Third Theory.

but it is not true that these customs and laws were administered unchanged. The *mallums* of the first race were not a stable institution. They were too much affected by the disorders of the times and the continual changes of boundries. Under the second race Charlemagne gave more complete forms to these assemblies, by combining

[1] Fayard, Aperçu Hist. sur le Parlement de Paris, vol. i.

[2] Guizot Hist. of Civ. in France, vol. iii, p. 278.

[3] Guizot, Hist. of Civ. in France, Lecture xi. Michelet, Orgines du Droit Français. Bastard d' Estang, Les Parl de France, vol. i, p. 44.

under one authority, territories previously ruled by many princes.
If these essemblies were the proto-type of any great institution
it naturally was of the States-General as Boullée well says:[1] "One
cannot prevent himself from thinking that the States-General
was inspired by the still recent recollections of the political
gatherings of Clovis and Charlemagne." When we consider
how the feudal system renewed all France; how it changed the
relation of man with man; how it affected the manners and ideas
of the people, no less than its laws and government, how can we
think that the Parliament of Paris should alone remain standing
in the midst of such an overthrow?[2] Institutions exist in society
which belong to all times, and without which a people, however
little civilized, could not endure for a day. Such are judicial
institutions. The same forms do not always exist; one which
has lost its power is replaced by another filled with youth and
strength, but society can not do without justice. It is not
surprising that historians have considered the successors of
different institutions as simple transformations of the same
institutions. Voltaire says:[3] " To represent a nation one must
be nominated by it, and removed at its pleasure," but the
magistrates of the Parliaments received their places from
the king, and held them at his will. Furthermore, to prove
their long descent, the Parliaments should possess some
of the attributes belonging to the assemblies of the old
dynasties; but they were only called upon to deliberate, con-

---

[1] Boullée, Hist. des Etats Généraux et autres Assemblies Représenta-
tives de France, depuis 1302 jusqu'en 1629.

[2] Beugnot, Comte de, Documents Inédits sur l' Hist. de Franc 1839.
Les Olim, vol. i. préface, p. 23. The last fifty years have been remarkably
fruitful in investigations and descoveries, shedding light upon the history
of France. The student of history has no more precious store-house of
new and valuable material than the magnificent " Collection de Documents
Inédits sur l' Histoire de France" still in course of publication by the
Ministry of Public Instruction.

[3] Essai sur les moeurs et l'esprit des nations.

cerning peace and war, or money grants. The whole spirit of their institution confined them to the administration of justice and the registration of edicts. Not until after the meeting of the Estates at Blois in 1576 do we find them asserting themselves to be the delegates of the States-General, and as such called to discuss great state interests, and this pretension rests upon a statement casually introduced.[1] The members. of the Parliament themselves were divided upon this question as numerous references prove.[2] The burden of proof seems to favor the theory that has become generally adopted by the jurists and historians of the 19th century that the Parliament of Paris is not the representation of the old national assemblies or *mallums*, not a special creation of any one king, but the outgrowth of the king's council. This charged at all times with the political affairs of the kingdom, by the extension of royal power and the increase of royal justice, was inevitably led to separate a section of the council and to devolve upon it the administration of justice. This section by the natural process of growth became the Parliament of Paris whose functions were legally recognized by the ordinance of Philippe le Bel.

---

[1] Boullée's Hist. des Etats Généraux, p. 59. "Il faut que tous édits soient verifiés et comme contrôlés ès cours de Parl."

[2] Fayard, Speech of Chancellor Oisie, vol. i, p. 1.
Boullée Etats Généraux, vol. i, p. 5.
Guizot, Hist. de France, vol. v, p. 216.

Composition of the Parliament of Paris.

To describe the organization of the Parliament of Paris, is to explain that of all others as they were modeled upon it. The Parliament was divided originally into three chambers; the Chambre des Requêtes which tried all cases instituted directly before the Parliament; the Chambre des Enquêtes, which had preliminary consideration of cases of appeal, and the Grand, Chambre, (identical with the Chambre aux Plaids), where appeals were finally heard and decided. Afterward was added the criminal chamber, or La Tournelle.

The Chambre des Requêtes, or Chamber of Petitions, existed from very early times,[1] and was organized to hear and answer petitions. Finally it considered most suits of original jurisdiction brought before the court.

Chambre des Requêtes.

During the last two centuries, it was especially occupied with "letters of committimus,"[2] which drew causes from all parts of France. The jury system had now entirely disappeared, but the number of judges in this Chamber partly atoned for the lack of the more popular element. Law suits were heard partly on oral, partly on written testimony. Decisions were not final, but could be appealed, either to the Chamber of Inquiry, or the Great Chamber.

The Chambre des Enquêtes, or Chamber of Inquiry, heard

---

[1] An edict of Nov. 1291, clearly refers to it.
[2] Sir J. Stephens, Lect: on Hist. of France, 212.

3

appeals from the Baillis, Prévôts, and other inferior tribunals. It
Chambre des. Enquêtes. took more especial cognizance of cases which were decided on written proof. The result of their deliberations was reported to the Great Chamber, where the decision was pronounced, sealed, and placed upon the registers. There were five Chambers of Inquiry in the Parliament of Paris, three in the Parliament of Toulouse, and two in the other parliaments. Their successive creation was brought about less by the multitude of law cases, than the necessity of procuring money, and hence the sale of new offices. [1]

The highest branch of the Parliament was the Great Chamber. Apart from the professional members of the court, La Grand' Chambre. the peers of France and the princesses of the blood had seats in this body. A member of the Parliament obtained admittance to the Great Chamber when he became the oldest member of the body to which he had been assigned on his entrance. All the plentitude of parliamentary authority centered in the Great Chamber. The judgments reached by the other sections were brought here for ratification. Matters of State as well as the highest legal questions were here discussed. The exceptional position of the Great Chamber of the Parliament of Paris at the capital of the kingdom, and its priority in age led it to arrogate to itself many cases which never occupied the provincial Parliaments. [2] At its dissolution in 1789, it was composed of forty-two active members; viz., the Premier Président, four senior Présidents-à-mortier, so styled from their caps, and thirty-seven counselors. The three Chambers were the great sections into which the Parliament of Paris was first divided. As its jurisdiction increased other subdivisions took place.

---

[1] Bastard d' Estang, Les Parl de France, vol. i, p. 204.

[2] Mérilhou, M. F., Les Parl. de France. Leur caractire politique depuis Philippe le Bel, jusqu'en, 1789. Paris, 1863, p. 18.

In 1380, during the reign of Charles VI, the usage was
introduced of submitting certain civil and criminal matters of
La Tournelle. slight importance to the judgment of a chosen
number of counselors. An edict of Francis I, 1515, formed
these into a Chamber with enlarged jurisdiction, and later it
acquired the exclusive right of considering all criminal cases, [1]
except the trials of nobles or great public officers. The members of the Tournelle varied from twenty to thirty and and were
furnished in rotation from the other Chambers in order, as it was
humanely stated, " that the habit of condemning men and
sentencing them to death should not alter the natural clemency
of the judges and render them inhuman." Some would derive
the name from this custom,[1] others[2] would obtain it from the
tower in which the criminal Chamber at Paris held its sittings.

The Grand Jours or Great Days were courts or commissions
of inquiry held at irregular intervals and for short periods of
Les Grand time by the special order of the king. A certain
Jours. number of parliamentary counselors were deputed to
take charge of these at the great cities within a certain jurisdiction. They had authority to summon all magistrates, to hear
complaints, to pursue the guilty, and if need be to pronounce
sentences of death. The decrees of the Grand Jours were executed directly, without appeal to the Parliaments.[3]

In the early days of Parliament in the interval from one
Parliament to another, judgments were rendered by commission-
La Chambre ers appointed by the king. A letter of Charles
des
vacations. VII, of 1454, enjoins upon the Parliament a sufficient
number of sessions, notwithstanding the vacations, to examine

[1] Desmaze, C., Le Parl. de Paris, vol. i.
[2] Bastard, vol. i, p. 345.
[3] Bastard, vol. i, p. 369.
Stephens, Lect. viii, p, 215.

the law suits that had accumulated. By degrees the Vacation Chamber assumed the form it retained, and annually on the ninth day of September it was opened by the Premier Président, who presided at its first session.[1]

The edict of May 1576, granting certain legal privileges to Huguenots, gave rise to Chambers that, with the exception of the Parliament of Paris, were composed half of Protestants, half of Catholics. This Parliament was not so generous in its acknowledgment of "the religion," as but one Protestant belonged to the section. These Chambers were suppressed by Louis XIV in Jan. 1669.[2]

Chambre de l'Edit.

The Marble Table decided all matters concerning rivers and forests, fishing and hunting. The name, the same in all the Parliaments, perpetuates the memory of the great marble table formed from a single slab in the Palais de Justice at Paris.

Table de Marbre.

The summary of the diverse jurisdictions of the Parliament would be incomplete were not the magistrates mentioned who formed the Ministerè Publique in the old sovereign courts. These law officers of the crown considered collectively were called the Parquet. They represented the king, then the very core of authority, and their duty was the enforcement of the penal law and the protection of the rights of the crown, or society at large. At the head of the Parquet was the Procureur Général, who had the superior direction of justice throughout all France. His functions were numerous. To him belonged all cases involving the rights of the king, care of the Royal Domain, titles of honor, punishment of oppression, and pursuit of criminals. He also had the oversight of prisons and of charitable and municipal organizations. Through him the king

Ministerè Publique.

---

[1] Desmaze, vol. i.
[2] Bastard, vol. i, p. 288.

communicated treatises, law projects and financial demands to the Parliament, and through him the Parliament signified to the king its willingness or unwillingness to act. When edicts were registered the Procureur Général gave his conclusion in writing; if a registration was denied, then the First Advocate General spoke in the king's presence to demand registration or order a Bed of Justice, for the curious distinction was made that "the Advocate of the king shall present all resolutions publicly proposed by speech, and all conclusions in writing shall be signed by the Procureur."[1] The "Gens du Roi" properly so called were the four superior officers, the Procureur, the First, Second and Third Advocate General, but the assistant officers of inferior rank were often classed with the "Gens du Roi." Any officer in his quality as "Gens du Roi" was privileged to speak with head covered and without interruption as he represented the king.

The Chancellor held the first position in the kingdom until the Revolution, and in the Parliament he had a voice and a seat
The Chan-
cellor. after the princes of the blood. Although strictly not belonging to the Parliament, he was considered a member and his influence was great.

The head of the Parliament was the Premier Président, and with him were associated nine Présidents-à-mortier, who were
The Prési-
dents. considered as representing him, and in his absence presided over the assembled Chambers.

---

[1] Bastard, vol. i, p. 296.

The Members.

The edict of 1302 divided the Parliament into three Chambers; an edict of 1374 fixed the number of its members at seventy-

Division into Chambers and apportionment of duties. eight counselors, forty-four ecclesiastics, thirty-four laymen and three presidents.[1] This number varied greatly at different epochs.

The sale of offices caused the needs of the treasury to be consulted more frequently than the necessities of justice. At the suppression of the Parliaments in 1789, the Parliament of Paris was divided into seven · Chambers, a Premier Président, nine Présidents-à-mortier, fifteen Présidents du Chambre, one hundred and fifty Counselors, a Procureur Général, three Avocats-Généraux and nine substitutes. Furthermore, there were two Greffiers-en-chef, or Registrars, twenty-five Commis-Greffiers or Assistant Registrars, and four Secretaries. Such was the great array of legal force which a single resolution on that eventful night in November, 1789, swept to the four winds.

An ordinance of Philippe le Long required the members of Parliament to reside at Paris. All the great church dignitaries were

Continued residence in Paris. at once excluded, save the Archbishop of Paris, and the Abbot of St. Denis, and all of the great lords who could not afford to maintain an establishment at Paris separate from their ancestral castles. Thus the lawyers were left in undisputed possession of the supreme court of justice.

The king at first assigned persons to sit for a session or at

---

[1] Dictionnaire de la Politique, Maurice Block, Paris, 1880, vol. ii, p. 503.

his pleasure, but by 1319 the practice obtained of appointing
Tenure of Offices. counselors for life. As late as 1467, however, there is
an edict of Louis XI, forbidding the removal of
judges, save for just cause. This makes it probable that there
was not entire freedom from arbitrary removal until after that
date.

A further concession was made to the power of the Parliament by permitting it to name a number of candidates to any
Sale of Offices. vacancy, from which the king made his choice. When
such places became a matter of sale, the king's power
of appointment was exercised without restraint. The offices of
Parliament were a constant temptation to a needy monarch. The
members enjoyed high consideration and opportunities for profit
were not wanting. The sale of judicial dignities can readily be
traced to the days of Philippe le Bel, but it was reserved
for the Father of his Country, Louis XII, to systematize the
practice and to recognize the profits as an annual source of
revenue. Francis I created a new Chamber with two Presidents
and eighteen Counselors. In the reign of Louis XIV, the office
of Président-à-mortier was sold for 500,000 francs, that of Counselor for 150,000 francs, that of Procureur Général for 700,000
francs.

The reign of the best of the Bourbons saw a further change.
M. Paulet,[1] secretary of the Parliament, advised a tax on official
Offices made Hereditary. incomes. Sully, who was casting about for ways to
raise money, eagerly adopted the suggestion. This
tax, the Paulette, was an assessment of one-sixtieth on the condition that the office should be made hereditary. Its owner
might sell it during his life time, or at his death it could be disposed of with his houses and lands. Ordinarily one of the sons

[1] Kitchin's Hist. of France, vol. ii, p. 459.
Mérilhou, M. F., Les Parl de France, p. 307.

took the place and thus were founded those judicial families
which formed a new order of nobility. This was an important
constitutional step, for it made the magisterial nobility a class.
The influence of this change remains to be seen. So acute an
observer as Montesquieu [1] defends the Paulette. It is certain
that a spirit of independence and of traditionary pride grew up in
these bodies, and tended to make them fearless administrators of
the powers entrusted to them. Count Bastard d'Estang, who
belonged to a parliamentary family that had had representatives
in the Parliament of Toulouse since the fourteenth century says:[2]
" The organization of the ancient French society, which, by the
incessant work of the individual elevated each generation beyond
the one that had preceded it, demanded the sacrifice of an entire
life time. Living in the certainty of the elevation of his
posterity the father prepared slowly and surely for the future of
his son, and France gained in stability." That there were evils
is certain. Judicial positions must often have been filled by
incompetent men, whose tastes and aptitudes were as unfitted to
the severe and monotonous labors of a counselor as were those
of Montaigne,[2] while they may not have had so promptly as did
he the good sense to resign their privileges and emoluments.
La Bruyère complains that youths hardly out of school passed
from the birch to the ermine. Furthermore, the Parliamentary
counselors who had paid for their offices, or inherited them, were
apt to consider themselves on the bench as the guardians of their
own interests and not as trustees of the rights of society. The
most serious evil came with the hereditary tenure of the office.

---

[1] Montesquieu, Esprit des Lois, liv. 5, chap. xix: "Cette vénalité est
bonne dans les états monarchiques, parce qu 'elle fait faire, comme un
mètier de famille, ce qu 'on ne voudrait pas entreprendre pour la vertu
qu 'elle distine chacun à son devoir, et rend les ordres de l' état plus
permanents."

[2] Bastard, vol. i, p. 138.

[3] Demogeot, Hist. de la Lit. Fran., p. 283.

Previously the members of Parliament had been the natural leaders of the Third Estate, hence forward, they were but another nobility whose sympathies were with the king that created and maintained them, not with the people and their constitutional privileges.

There must have been, however, strong influences toward justice and uprightness to produce so illustrious a body of men as the French magistracy. What country can point to a judge more incorruptible and loyal than[1] Achille de Harlay, more courageous and unflinching than Matthieu Molé,[2] more learned, wise and influential than d' Aguesseau?[3] Beugnot says:[4] "The memorable services rendered the country, by the Parliament of Paris, and the hereditary virtues of its members were the sources of the authority which it exercised our minds as well as over the affairs of State." Bastard declares:[5] "If anything can inspire veneration for our ancient magistracy, it is intimate acquaintance with their daily life." Certain it is, that in the early days of Parliament, the faults of the members were

Lives of the Magistrates.

---

[1] Achille de Harlay, First President of Parliament of Paris in 1582. He was noted for his learning and integrity, and firmly opposed the designs of the League Nouvelle Biographie Générale.

[2] Molé, Matthieu, First President during the war of the Fronde; conspicuous for his intrepidity in quelling the insurrection. Mémoires de Cardinal de Retz. Portraits.

[3] D' Aguesseau, "a man who did honor to France by his virtues, his profound and varied learning, and his enlightened views on jurisprudence." La Harpe, Cours de Lit., tome xiv, chap. 1.

[4] Beugnot, Document inédits, Les Olim, préface p. iii.

[5] Bastard's Parl. de France, vol. i, p. 199.
Sir Henry Maine, Ancient Law, p. 79. "The French jurists formed the best instructed and nearly the most powerful class in the nation. In all the qualities of the advocate, the judge and legislator, they far excelled their compeers throughout Europe."
De Tocqueville. The Old Regime and the Revolution, chap. 11.
"No doubt the Parliaments thought more of themselves than of the public good, but when it was necessary to defend their independence, and their honor, they were always intrepid, and gave heart to those who surrounded them."
Also, cf. Mérilhou, Les Parl. de France, p. 243, and Baird's Rise of the Huguenots in France, vol. i, p. 334.

4

faithfully corrected. An ordinance of 1318 forbids the counselors to eat or drink with those who had suits before them, and further enjoins upon them to attend the sessions and to leave their seats but once in the morning. It then adds, "It is a great disgrace that while the court is in session, its members should be frolicing and walking about the halls of the Palace." We may fear, however, that the ordinance was not always effective, for the witty President ̧de Harlay, descendent of the great de Harlay, once caustically remarked that "if the gentlemen of the court who talked would make no more noise than those who slept, it would be a great favor to those who listened " Louis XIV. himself did not disdain to inform Chancellor Le Tellier that he had seen the judges on their way to the Palace with cravats, gray clothes, and canes in their hands, and they must be admonished that such a costume was unbecoming a magistrate.

This was indeed in contrast to the usual magnificence affected by the members. The richness of the costumes worn often Costumes of the Magistrates. excited the ridicule of philosophers and satirists.[1] At the morning sessions from All Saints Day to the Annunciation of the Virgin, the presidents sat in an ermine robe and cap; the remainder of the year they were arrayed in a scarlet robe. The counselors and advocates wore red robes with large sleeves adorned with velvet. The clerks of the counselors wore violet robes. In the afternoon meetings all were arrayed in black gowns.

In the seignorial courts no fees were demanded, but when lords and bishops were succeeded by legists, fixed compensation Remuneration of the Magistrates. became needful. The oldest document concerning the wages of the magistrates is an account of 1301, preserved in the archives of Florence, which says that the seigneur presiding over the Parliament shall receive ten sous per

---

[1] Bastard vol. i, p. 166.

day, while the court is in session. In 1400 the First President had
one thousand livres a year; [1] in the reign of Louis XIV, twelve
thousand livers. At each date the salary of a Président-à-mortier
was one-half these respective sums. Gifts were naturally given
by the grateful or anxious suitor, which at length became an
established usage, and were known by the suggestive name of
" épices," or "sweetmeats." Finally, they became fixed in pro-
portion to the labor involved, and in the eyes of justice and
legislation were entirely legitimate fees, as the stated salaries
were small and often poorly paid. Society recompensed the
magistrates by consideration, and kings by honors and privileges;
at the opening of the great movement which closed their existence, they were in full possession of all the privileges and
exemptions of the nobility.

Nearly all the Parliaments re-opened November 12th. The
day was announced at Toulouse by loud peals from the tower
Opening of clock, which rang only on this occasion and at the ob-
Parl. sequies of one of its members. The day was observed
at Paris by elaborate ceremonies.

The counselors began their duties at early hours. At
Toulouse, the Palace was opened at five o'clock, but finally at
Hours of Toulouse and Paris the opening hour became six
opening. o'clock. Mondays, Thursdays and Fridays the Great
Chamber met and continued in session until 10 a. m. The order of
business was unvarying. From 6 a. m. until 7 a. m. reports were
heard; at 7 a. m. the arguments of cases began, and with a short in-
termission for breakfast, was continued until 10 a. m.; then reports
were made, consultations were given, and other miscellaneous business transacted. Tuesdays and Saturdays, afternoon sessions were
held. Wednesdays and Saturdays were reserved for important
matters connected with State policy and registrations, when the

About $1,400 of our money, and far more in purchasing power.

Great Chamber sat with closed doors. In the eighteenth century these early hours had not changed, and the notorious case of the Diamond Necklace called together one hundred and eighty-seven members, for nine months at the early morning hour, listening to testimony and arguments to vindicate a queen.

Great interest always attaches to local surroundings, and the places where the great ceremonies of the ancient magistracy took

Palais de place deserve description. In several provinces the
Justice. . kings had given to the Parliament one of their palaces. These assumed and retained the name "Palais de Justice." Two of these palaces are of great antiquity and abound in historical reminiscence. The Palais de Justice of Toulouse had been inhabited by the ancient kings and counts of Toulouse, and traditions said that Roman magistrates had pronounced decisions on this site. [1] The Palais de Justice of Paris is an old kingly residence on a little island formed by the Seine, in the heart of old Paris. St. Louis gave it for the use of the Parliament, and Philippe-le-Bel greatly enlarged it, so it was reputed in his day one of the most beautiful works of architecture in the world. The general assemblies of all the Chambers was held in the hall of St. Louis. No single hall in the world unless it be the great oaken hall at Westminister, has witnessed such varied and tragic scenes. On more than one occasion the Parliament in this place maintained the rights and nationality of France against the intrigues and disloyalty of great nobles.[8] Here in 1589 Président Le Maître declared "that no treaty shall be made for the transfer of the State and crown of France to foreign princes." Here the little king Louis XIV. was taken when five years old to assure the Parliament of his good will, and here a

[1] Bastard, Parl. de France, vol. i, p. 184.
[9] Antiquités de Paris, p. 135.
[8] Guizot, Hist. de France, vol. v, p. 52.

dozen years later he treated it with a contumely that was never forgotten. Here during the war of the Fronde a price was set on Mazarin's head, and his fine library of four thousand volumes was offered for sale to pay the reward.[1] Here Président de Mesmes administered a well merited rebuke to the Prince of Conti, who had introduced an envoy from Spain to treat against the king of France. " What! is it possible that a prince of the blood should propose to give a seat upon the fleurs-de-lis to the most cruel enemy of the fleurs-de-lis?" What whirligig of time could present a greater contrast than this same hall when the stately Presidents and the gorgeously-robed advocates were succeeded by the Sans-Culottes of the Revolutionary Tribunal. The great hall was re-christened La Salle d' Egalité, and a court of judges was formed, which to the grave and learned counselors of other days would have seemed the veriest rabble. The populace of Paris flowed in and out while Marie Antoniette was sentenced to death for the crime of being a queen,[2] and they looked on in astonished silence as the twenty-two Girondists who were to die on the morrow, marched forth singing the Marseillaise. [3] From here Camille Desmoulins, Mme. Roland, and finally Robespierre himself, the Terror incarnate, went forth in turn to the same fatal doom. [4]" The hall has been sadly changed. The visitor who gazes at reputable appearing advocates in gowns and caps, sharp-featured notaries, uneasy clients and wearied judges, sees little to bring back the Parliament of Paris or the Revolutionary Tribunal. The voice of Danton has ceased to vibrate, the eloquence of Harlay no longer delights the ear. The prose of the nineteenth century has replaced the pathos of the eighteenth, the pride and dignity of the seventeenth."

1 Guizot, Hist. de France, vol. v, p. 859.
2 Thiers' Hist. of French Revolution, vol. iii, p. 196.
3 Martin H., Hist. de France, vol. vi, p. 612.
4 Am. Law Rev., Parl. in France, vol. xii, p. 262.

¹ Jean de Montluc, a Counselor under St. Louis, had for his own use made a record of the most ancient edicts and most important decisions. In 1257 he was appointed "greffier-civil," or Registrar to the court. The oldest "greffes," or registers, are called the "Olim," because the third volume begins with the words "Olim Homines de Bayona." From the great utility of these registers in giving access to ancient law, the thought arose that nothing had the force of law unless contained in them. Gradually it became a custom, then an indispensable formality, to inscribe all edicts in the books of Parliament. Philippe le Bel, who had a keen sense of financial value, sold these volumes to "good and worthy people," and many a monarch after him thought a favor well recompensed by the gift of an important "greffe." Not until the time of Colbert were these records collected at the Palais de Justice. The sagacious minister knew well their importance and did what he could to repurchase the volumes, which formed many a valuable heirloom. Some that had been retained at the Palais de Justice had been burned in the fire of 1618, and at the present time the collection is quite incomplete.

The Registers or Olim.

The Parliaments.

The edict of Philippe le Bel, of 1302, had ordained that "for the convenience of his subjects, and the expedition of law cases there should be held each year, two sessions of the Parlia-

¹ Bastard's Hist. des Parl., vol. i, p. 326.
Voltaire, Parl. de Paris, ed. 1769, p. 56.
Desmaze, C., Le Parl. de Paris, vol. 1.

ment of Paris, two Exchequers of Rouen, two Grand Jours at Troyes, and a session of the Parliament at Toulouse."[1]

The date of organization, and the founder of each Parliament, so far as accurately known, are given in the following list: [2]

Paris,	1302						Philippe le Bel.
Toulouse,	$\begin{Bmatrix} 1302 \\ 1444 \end{Bmatrix}$		Before Charles VII the history not well known.
Grenoble,	1453						Charles VII.
Bordeaux,	1462						Louis XI.
Dijon,	1476						Charles VII.
Rouen,	1499						Louis XII.
Aix,	1501						Louis XII.
Pau,	1519						Francis I.
Rennes,	1553						Francis II.
Metz,	1633						Louis XIII.
Besançon,	1674						Louis XIV.
Douai,	1686						Louis XIV.
Nancy,	1774						Louis XV.

The organization of the Parliament of Paris, its system of administering justice and its judicial rights and privileges were the model after which the others were formed. They differed from it only in those variations which local and peculiar causes required.

Although Parliaments were instituted by kings, they considered themselves the protectors of the rights of the province

Parliament as Guardian of the Province. of provinces within the bounds of their authority. The whole of the eighteenth century was marked by struggles to maintain their independence. Furthermore, no province was was considered as finally annexed to France until it had been placed under the jurisdiction of one of these sovereign courts.

After several changes in custom and opinion, the position was at length taken, that each Parliament was the sovereign court

---

[1] " Propter commodum subditorum nostrorum et expeditionem causarum, proponimus ordinare quod duo Parlamenta Parisiis, duo Scacaria Rotomagi, dies Trecenses bis tenebuntur in anno, et quod Parlamentum Tolosae tenebitur sicut solebat teneri temporibus retroactis."

[2] Bastard, vol. ii, p. 103.
Desmaze, vol. i, table, p. 1.

All Parlia-
ments
Sovereign.
within its own precinct. No appeal could be made even to the Parliament of Paris, and decisions made by any Parliament were to be executed in all parts of the kingdom.

Gradually the doctrine arose that the Parliaments, taken collectively, formed one great judicial institution, all of whose members had equal privileges and inter-community of rights.[1] The Parliament of Paris was the first Class, and all together constituted a single body, which represented the kingdom of France. If this pretension had been generally admitted, the form of government would have been transferred from an hereditary king to an assembly of hereditary magistrates.

Parliaments
as classes.

The Legislative and Political Rights.

Having studied the Parliaments as judicial organizations, there remains the explanation of the legislative and political power, with which time, custom and the tacit consent of both nation and monarch had invested them. There are a number of obvious reasons why this body of magistrates should at length find themselves clothed with an authority to which the judicial history of no other country can furnish a parallel.

To a certain extent legislative power had been conferred upon it. Whenever a royal law was defective in any detail, the Parliament could issue an arrêt or decision supplying this defect [2] The arrêt was provisional only until the

Legislative
Power.

---

[1] Voltaire, Parl. de Paris, chap. lxvi.
[2] Mérilhou, M. F., Les Parl. de France, p. 452.

king himself should remedy the fault; still, the right of making such amendments was a legislative privilege of high value, and under more favorable circumstances might have served as the entering wedge to secure for the Parliament of Paris the broader privileges of its namesake across the Channel.

We have tried to prove that the Parliament of Paris was a section of the king's council, set aside to consider judicial ques-

Heirs of King's Council.

tions. As the clerks and lawyers gradually replaced the barons and prelates, they tenaciously held to all the privileges of those who preceded them, one of the most valuable of which was the consideration of questions of state.

We have seen how the Parliament gradually laid claim to bring the representative of the States-General,[1] and what recogni-

Representing States-General.

tion was given this pretension by the assembly at Tours. As such, during the long intervals which separated the sessions of the States-general, it claimed the character of guardian of the rights vested in those assemblies.

We have also seen that registration came to be considered as an indispensable ceremony, giving validity to laws, until the

Registration and Remonstrance.

principle was admitted without question that no Parliament was bound to execute any ordinance until it had first been communicated to it, and entered upon its records. When the ancient kings desired to make important modifications in the general legislation of the kingdom, they had been wont to ask the Parliament to examine the project and report their observations upon it. The first time that these observations took the form of "remonstrances," was in the address sent by the Parliament to Louis XI, touching the Pragmatic Sanction. [2] This right of observation and remonstrance was one of the most essential portions of the political power of Parliament. If a

---

[1] Mérilhou, M. F., Les Parl. de France, p. 454.
[2] Voltaire, Le Parlement de Paris, chap. 11. "Remontrances touchant les Priviléges de l' E glise gallicane.
5

remonstrance was unheeded the next step was to request the king to withdraw the ordinance. If this was refused, Parliament formally declined to register it among the records. This refusal was only overcome by "lettres de jussion," or a compulsory demand. If still registration was withheld a Bed of Justice[1] was called. Then the king appeared in all his majesty, and from the summit of his throne of justice, commanded that the edict should be inscribed in the records. When the court was thus obliged to submit, the decree of registration was preceded by a preamble, stating that the decree was registered " by the king's express command," and this protest was entered upon the records. If the right of resistance did not actually prevail it was asserted, and every new assertion was supposed to add to its strength.

The constant opposition of the Parliaments of Paris to the encroachments of the Court of Rome, was the greatest political
Registration of Pope's Bull. service it ever rendered. By refusing registration, and by remonstrating, Parliament succeeded in establishing a right to intervene in ecclesiastical affairs, and won for itself the name of the bulwark of the liberties of the Gallican Church.[2] Before the statute of Praemunire was passed in England, forbidding appeals from the king's court to the Court of Rome, [3] an advocate of the Parliament of Paris, Pierre de Cunières, had in 1329 proposed this remedy against the usurpations of the Church.

---

[1] Desmaze C, vol. i, p. 119. "Lit de Justice," signifies the throne upon which the king was seated. It was formed of five cushions, one serving as a seat, another as a back, two as arm supports, and one as a foot-stool.

Bastard, Les Parl. de Fr., voi. i, p. 19.

It has been said that "Lits de Justice" were so named, because then justice slept; i. e., the king's person united both legislative and judicial power. However, this designation also came from the arrangement of the throne.

[2] Voltaire, Parl. de Paris, 1769, chap. 10.

[3] Stubbs, Constitutional Hist. of England, vol. ii, p. 410. "The first statute of Praemunire was an ordinance of 1353."

The Parliament also established a right to a voice in diplomatic questions. All treaties with foreign powers, before Registration of Treaties becoming effective, required registration, and so were subject to the observations, remonstrances and refusals of the court. However, this right figures on few occasions which are historically important, and these few clearly prove the real impotence of the proud tribunal, when met by the positive wishes of a strong monarch. When Francis I. desired to be freed from the humiliating engagement of the Treaty of Madrid, he called a meeting of the Parliament of Paris, at which were present deputations from the six other existing Parliaments. He gravely laid before them the provisions of the treaty, which a few days before he had sworn by his royal oath to fulfill. He asked their consideration of it, and their opinion as to registration. They as gravely replied that "neither the treaty, nor the royal oath were binding; the former not having been the act of the king; the latter having been exacted from him when in bondage; that therefore he should neither give up Burgundy, nor return into Spain." [1] One simple-minded counselor, Bishop Poncher, whodid not understand this little comedy, was so imprudent as to give it as his opinion, that Francis should go back to Spain. He thereby brought upon himself, a prison and death.[2]

The peculiar institution of the Ministère Publique and its connection with the Parliament, enabled the latter to prefer pretensions to political power, which were sometimes Ministère Publique successful. The Procureur général, the chief of the Parquet, had so important and so diverse functions, that his influence was felt in every branch of administration, and as one of the most powerful members of the Parliament, the latter often identified itself with his exercise of power. [3]

---

[1] Kitchin's Hist. de France, vol. ii, page 209.
[2] The account most favorable to Francis I, concerning the treaty of Madrid is found in Duruy, Hist. de France, vol. ii.
[3] Vicomte de Bastard d' Estang. Les Parl. de France, vol. i, p. 297.

When the Parliament of Paris was consolidated by Philippe le Bel, he had no thought of making it a judge in great affairs of State. The trial of the Knights Templars in 1309, which assuredly would have come before it in later times was held by the commissioners of Pope Clement V. The first time that the Parliament uttered a formal remonstrance was during the reign of Louis XI, concerning the famous Pragmatic Sanction of Bourges.[1] During the reign of his son, Charles VIII, great weight was evidently attached to the attitude of Parliament on political questions, for the Duke of Orleans, afterward Louis XII, desiring to obtain the regency, and the government of the young king laid his wishes before the assembled counselors and asked them to declare in his favor. The First President responded: "Parliament renders justice for the people; finances, wars, and the care of kings are not within its province."[2] Not always was this body governed by such modest and discreet sentiments.

The reign of Louis XII was not marked by the slightest difference between the monarch and his high tribunal. Two noteworthy ordinances held in esteemed repute, are inseparably associated with his name. The first enacted that no Baillis or Prévôt should be permitted to act as judge, unless he was able to read and had studied law. Voltaire wittily says: "The high officials, all of whom were nobles, preserved their dignity and

---

[1] Voltaire, Le Parlement de Paris, 1769, p. 155.

[2] Quoted by Voltaire in chap. 12.

ignorance, and lettered lieutenants of lesser birth judged in their names."[1]

The second edict of 1499, goes far to explain the title gratefully given him, the Father of his Country. " Qu'on suive toujours la loi malgré les ordres contraires à la loi, que l'importunité pourrait arracher du monarque."

During the reign of Francis I, the Parliament of Paris became an important factor in political events.[2] Its first variance

Francis I, and Parliament.
with the king arose over the Concordat.[3] Francis I, who had need of Leo **X**, abolished the Pragmatic Sanction, which had so far secured to the Church in France, greater liberties than were enjoyed in any country in Europe. He substituted for it the Concordat, by which he gave the pope certain portions of the Church revenue, and appropriated to himself the right to appoint to benefices; in other words, the king presented the pope with the wealth of the Church, and the pope handed over to the king its independance. " Each gave to the other, what belonged to neither." [4]The struggle over the registration of the Concordat was hard and long. The king indignantly insisted on registration, and at a Bed of Justice protested that no Parliament should make him a Doge of Venice. After twelve years of strife the infamous Du Prat removed ecclesiastical matters from the cognizance of Parliament, and handed them over to the king's council.[5] The other acts of this reign are not so creditable. It broke the treaty of Madrid, attainted the king's enemy and kinsman, Charles of Bourbon,

[1] Voltaire, Le Parl de Paris, chap. 15.
[2] Mérilhou, Les Parl. de France, et leur caractère politique depuis Philippe le Bel, jusqu'en, 1789. p p. 135, 224.
[3] The text of the Concordat is given in full in the Recueil gen des anc. lois. xii, 75-97.
[4] Bastard d' Estang, vol. ii, p. 9.
Baird, The Rise of the Huguenots. Vol. i, p. 37.
[5] Kitchin, vol. ii, p. 182.

and sanctioned the persecutions of the Huguenots. The reigns
of Henry II, Charles IX, and Henry III, were marked by a
constant succession of conflicts between the king and the Parliament, with a monotonous sameness of result. [1]These two powers
agreed on only one matter, and this was hatred of the Huguenots.
The horrors of St. Bartholomew drew forth from this high judicial
body an approving edict, ordering a yearly procession of thanks-
giving to celebrate the great victory of the faith. Fortunately
the change in public sentiment spared France this disgrace.
Henry IV, knew well how to manage this company of magistrates, and manage them he did, firmly and sensibly. When
Henry IV, and Parliament. they refused to register the Edict of Nantes, he
summoned to the Louvre deputies from all the
Chambers.[2] "What I have done," he said, "is for the good of
peace. I speak to you not in royal robe, or with sword and cape,
but as a father of his family conversing freely with his children.
I ask you to register the edict I have granted the Protestants.
God has chosen to give me this kingdom, which is mine by birth
and conquest. You, gentlemen of Parliament, would not be in
your seats but for me. If obedience was due to my predecessors,
it is much more due to me." [3] When a father addresses his
children in such terms, he is generally obeyed. The edict was
speedily registered. With Richelieu and the minority of
Louis XIII, came again stormy times. In 1615 the Parliament
without the royal order, dared to summon princes, dukes, peers
Richelieu and Parliament. and high officials to deliberate upon the needs of the
state, and the relief of the people. "We," it said,
" hold the place in council of the princes and barons, who, from

[1] Baird, The Rise of the Huguenots. Vol. i, p. 237.
[2] Guizot, Hist. de France, vol. v, p. 112.
[3] Mérilhou, M. F., Les Parl. de France, p. 303. "Cette manifestation
d' une autorité nouvelle dut faire une perfonde impression sur les magis-
trats."

time immemorial were near the person of the king."[1] This assumption Richelieu constantly fought against. He would not allow the pretension of magistrates to meddle in affairs of State. There was constant altercation between the king and Richelieu on the one side, and Parliament on the other, whether about points of jurisdiction or the registration of edicts respecting finances. On one of these occasions[2] the entire Parliament was ordered to the Louvre, and there with bare heads and on bended knees was compelled to supplicate the king's forgiveness. This humiliating experience was not sufficient to restrain their assertions of right and authority and the struggles continued for ten years longer, when in 1641 the king issued an edict prohibiting the Parliament from any interference in affairs of State and administration, the preamble of which is as formal a declaration of absolute power as any ever promulgated by Louis XIV. The Cardinal had at last gained the victory. The attempts of Parliament at independence during the wars of the Fronde, only demonstrated how futile was its authority, and how completely was it the tool of the uppermost faction. Guizot says:[3] "The pretensions of the magistrates were often foundationless; the restless and meddlesome character of their assemblies did harm to their remonstrances; but for a long while they maintained in the teeth of more and more absolute kingly power, the country's rights in the government, and they had perceived the dangers of that sovereign monarchy which certainly sometime raises States to the highest pinnacle of their glory, but only to let them sink before long to a condition of the most grievous abasement." Louis XIV never forgot the part that Parliament played during the stormy scenes of the Fronde, in the early years of his boyhood. He had that instinctive apprehension of the existence of latent

Louis XIV, and Parliament.

---

[1] Guizot, Hist. de France, vol. ii, p. 195.
[2] Voltaire, Hist. du Parl. de Paris, vol. v, chap. 49, May 12, 1631.
[3] Guizot, Hist. de France, vol. v, p. 220.

power that led him to give an effectual check to the aspirations of this assembly at the very outset of his kingly career.

In the year 1615 the Parliament had refused to register certain financial edicts. The king (a boy not yet eighteen years of age) presented himself before the assembly in hunting attire, booted and spurred and, as is commonly added, with riding-whip in his hand. He haughtily commanded the Parliament to address no more remonstrances to him, but to confine themselves to the strict discharge of their duties. In 1673 he issued an ordinance declaring that all royal edicts should be registered within eight days from their date by the Parliament of Paris, and within six weeks by the other Parliaments of France.[1] We hear no more of the political role of Parliament during this long reign. In the period of struggle between Bousset and Louis XIV on one side, and Rome and Innocent XI on the other, the Parliaments vied emulously in the support of the king's policy. Louis, satisfied with the apparent submission of the supreme court, placed his last will and testament in their custody, where it was deposited in a small room built expressly for its safe keeping. He seems to have argued that a body so submissive during his life-time would continue to be so after his death. But how quickly they took their revenge for the contumely of long silence. While his body was still lying in state at Versailles, the Parliament assembled without having been convoked,[2] and measures were at once taken to break the will of the dead king. A few words from Orleans to the Parliament sufficed. The Duke received from the Parliament the regency during the king's minority, and the Parliament received from this imprudent depository of royal authority the political power of which it had been deprived for sixty

[1] Sir J. Stephens, Lect. on Hist. of France, p. 225.
[2] Guizot, Hist. de France, vol. vi, p. 54.
Mémoires de Saint-Simon, Derniers moments de Louis XIV. Hachette edition.

41

The Missis sippi Com- pany. years. The part which the Parliament took in resist- ing the chimerical projects of the Scotchman Law reflect great credit upon it. The opposition was probably due more to the repugnance which this body ever showed to novel ideas, than to its comprehension of the pernicious results of Law's system. It had forbidden the introduction of printing under Louis XI, it had condemned the philosophy of Descartes in 1624, it had opposed the establishment of the French Academy by Richelieu, [1] and from similar motives it now remon- strated against the financial innovations of Law.

The two great questions with which the Parliaments are identified during the 18th century, are the controversies concern- ing the papal bull " Unigenitus" and the expulsion of the Jesuits.

The long quarrel between the Jansenists and the Jesuits 'was fanned into fresh flame by the final publication of the Pope's bull, which quoted one hundred and one propositions from the work of Père Quesnel and condemned them as heretical. The bull Unigenitus appeared Sept. 8, 1713, and was registered by the express wish of Louis XIV, Feb. 14, 1714. The dying king, troubled and alarmed by discussions he deemed hurtful to true religion, desired to see the kingdom at peace before his death; but for fifty years the bull Unigenitus was a fruitful cause of dispute and resistance between Parliament and the Church, while the court party veered from one side to another as selfish interest dictated. During the first years of the regency the Duke of Orleans abandoned the Jesuits to the indignation of the people, and the bull was practically a dead letter, but in 1720 the unprincipled Dubois desired to become a cardinal, and so offered his good services to the Papal court. Voltaire says, with scornful disdain, both for the question at issue and the conduct of the Archbishop: "The greater part of these proposi-

The Bull Uni- genitus.

---

[1] Voltaire, Hist. du Parl. De Paris, chap. 51.

6

tions condemned by the bull Unigenitus concerned metaphysical
questions about free-will, which the Jansenists no more understood than the Jesuits. The Archbishop had more contempt for
the bull than all the Parliaments of the kingdom, but he would
have tried to force the Koran upon the Church if the Koran
could have advanced his interests."[1] Therefore, Dec. 4, 1720,
after stormy resistance on the part of the Parliament, and a threat
from the Regent to replace it by another tribunal, the bull was
again registered.

The controversy was by no means extinguished. The middle
classes throughout the country sided strongly with the Jansenists, and eargerly seized every opportunity to testify
their opinion. In 1730 Louis XV held a Bed of Justice, and enforced a third registration of the papal edict. The
next day the Parliament met and drew up protests and petitions,
and for two years the judicial business was neglected, while the
counselors passed their time in agitating and framing new
remonstrances. The people became excited to a degree of
extravagant fanaticism. Miracles were produced in abundance
to witness to the truths of Jansenius. The tomb of one of the
Jansenist saints in the cemetery of St. Médard became noted as
the seat of miraculous cures, and so disturbing were the scenes
enacted there that government was compelled to interfere and
shut out the public. Then it was some profane wit wrote over
the gate:

The Contest
Continued.

"De par le Roi, défense à Dieu,
De faire miracle en ce lieu."

A final struggle was brought about by the order of the
Archbishop of Paris in 1749, in which he commanded his priests
to require each dying person to affirm belief in the bull *Unigenitus*, before receiving the last sacraments of the Church; other-
wise Christian burial was denied.

[1] Voltaire, Hist. du Parl. de Paris, chap. 61.

Now, indeed, all orders and parties were embroiled, and the very foundations of society were shaken. The Bishops throughout the country issued pastoral letters against the Parliaments, and the Parliaments ordered the letters to be publicly burned, These were dangerous times for the Parliaments and the Church to be indulging in open and bitter controversy. The attention of the people was called as never before to the rights of government and the relations of Church and State, and the writings of Rousseau[1] just now appearing, were awakening passionate enthusiasm.

In 1753, the members of the Parliament of Paris were banished, and a Provisional Court was formed, but such determined opposition was awakened that the king recalled them. Again, the magistracy were exiled, and again recalled, but in the sympathy aroused by the attack of an assassin upon the king, the Parliament only returned by giving a pledge to desist from further attacks upon the bull. Outward hostility ceased, but discontent and anger smouldered beneath the surface.

They finally found expression in the blow aimed against the Order of Jesuits. The accumulated hatred of the magistracy and
Expulsion of the Jesuits. the popular party throughout the country, aided by the attacks of the sceptical Encyclopædists led by Voltaire and Diderot, brought about the measures, which terminated in the ordinance of August 2, 1762. This decree abolished the Society of Jesus in France, secularized its members, and confiscated its property.

[1] Rousseau "that remarkable man who, without learning, with few virtues, and no strength of character, has nevertheless stamped himself ineffaceably on history by the force of a vivid imagination, and by the help of a genuine and burning love for his fellowmen, for which much will always have to be forgiven him."

For the effect of the writings of Rousseau on the history of his time, see Sir Henry Maine, Ancient Law, p. 83.

De Tocqueville, The Ancient Régime, chap. 13.
Demogeot, Hist. de La Lit. Fran., p. 506.
Van Laun, H., Hist. of French Lit., vol. iii, pp. 90-111.
Saintsbury, G., Hist. of French Lit., Clarendon Press, 1882, p. 484.

Fruitless altercation had too familiarized the magistracy to a system of obstruction. More than forty years of the reign of Louis XV. had passed in a ceaseless struggle between the judicial power and the crown. [1] The needs of the Treasury, increased by war, constantly compelled new financial edicts, and refusals of registration were met by frequent Beds of Justice. This anarchy could not endure; either the crown must resume its authority, or the Parliament would control the State.

Louis aroused himself from his lethargy, and for once acted vigorously and expeditiously. Further compromise was no longer considered. By the advice of Chancellor Maupeou, the king took the extreme step of suppressing altogether the ancient Parliaments of the realm, both in the capital and the provinces. To take their place six new tribunals were instituted Feb. 23, 1771, under the name of conseils-supérieurs, in the towns of Arras, Blois, Châlons-sur-Marne, Clermont, Lyons, and Poitiers, the central court of justice being still maintained at Paris. This great organic change was not accomplished without obstinate resistance on the part of the Parliaments and expostulations even from the princes of the blood; but the great mass of the people looked on indifferently. The privileges and immunities of the Parliaments had lost them their hold upon the third estate, and their later contentions with the crown were regarded as so many selfish struggles for their own aggrandizement.

Suppression of the Parliaments

To recommend the new courts to public favor, Maupeou announced that justice would now be administered free of expense, and the sale of offices was forbidden.

When the new king ascended the throne he re-established the Parliaments; but they had learned no wisdom from their exile. After fourteen years, Louis XVI found himself in the

---

[1] Bastard, Les Parl. de France, vol. ii, p. 406.

same situation as the king, his grandsire, facing refractory counselors.

They continued to make angry remonstrances about registering money loans, and the king was obliged to use the despotic measure of a Bed of Justice. The Parliament doubtless thought it was conciliating public opinion, which was averse to new taxes, but the needs of the Treasury were urgent and its demands continued. Finally the Parliament of Paris declared that according to the ancient constitution of France, the establishment of new imposts belonged only to the States-General. It little anticipated that this cry meant its own destruction.

The States-General, transformed into the Constituent Assembly, had scarcely existed four months when the great Dissolution tribunals ceased to be. [1] Nov. 3, 1789, Alexander of Parliaments Lameth moved the abolition of the Parliaments. "They are now in vacation," objected some one. "So much the better," shouted Mirabeau, "Let them remain there; they will pass from sleep to death, and there will be no return." The decree, voted with cries of joy by the majority, declared that the Parliaments should be in perpetual vacation. Temporary courts were at once organized, and iu September, 1791, new judicial organizations were framed.

Thus the Parliaments of France passed out of history.

[1] Bastard, Les Parl. de France, vol. ii, p. 642.
Martin, H., Hist. de France, vol. vi, chap. 4.

Parliamentary Development in France and England.

A final question now remains: Why did the Curia Regis of France, the King's Council of Philippe Auguste, eventuate solely in a judicial body, dependant for its existence upon the king's favor, and hampered by its lack of legal foundation, while the Curia Regis of England of the[1] same century, the King's Council of Henry II advanced steadily toward the parliamentary system of the fifteenth,[2] the seventeenth and the nineteenth centuries?

The answer rests partly upon racial characteristics that are real elements in historical development. Freeman says:[3] "The institutions of a people are the natural growth of the circumstances under which it finds itself." Surely, the distinguishing attribute of race is a potential circumstance. These qualities, which each generation receives from its predecessors, and transmits to the generation following, form the most s table portion of our physical, mental and moral being and beneath every political variation, they must be sought for and will be found.

For over fifteen centuries[4] Great Britain was peopled and governed exclusively by members of the great Teutonic family; there was an undisturbed development of German habits of thought and mind. In France throughout the same period, there

Difference in Race.

---

[1] Stubbs, Const. Hist. of England, vol. i, p. 388.
[2] Stubbs, Const. Hist. of England, vol. ii, p. 161.
[3] Freeman, E. A., Comparative Politics, p. 30. This is Montesquieu's theory, although he underrates the strength of inherited qualities. Cf. Chapters 14, 15, 23 and 29, of "Esprit des Lois."
[4] Greene's Making of England. Introduction, note 15. "The first recorded appearance of the Saxons off the coast of Gaul, and in the Channel was in A.D. 287."

was a vast preponderance of the Gallic, or Roman-Gallic over
the Teutonic element of society. After the German invasion of
the fifth century, the country remained divided among half
savage tribes that took on no distinctive aspect of nationality,
until the strong hand of Charlemagne held them in his grasp.
Then followed the slow and imperfect fusion of different races
that were not welded into one nation of Frenchmen, until the
Hundred Year's War was completed.[1] Sir James Stephen says:
" England has so long successfully maintained her free institutions, because she is still as she has always been, German; because
her national franchises are the spontaneous and legitimate fruit of
her national character; of that character dutiful, serious, persever-
ing, reverential and hopeful, which has been transmitted to us
from our Anglo-Saxon ancestors."

England has ever been governed by English law, " a body
of opinions, maxims, and moral sentiments, which it would be
difficult to define," and that has largely grown out
Difference of Law. of judicial decisions, and early German and English
customs.[2] Roman law has affected English law[3] in so far as it has
stimulated a judicial and legal spirit, produced activity in legislation and incited an orderly and systematic arrangement of laws,
and of methods of legal procedure; but the body of English
legislation has remained essentially the same from the ninth to
the nineteenth century. Never has the law been wrested by
any one class to be used as a tool to manipulate its own interest;

---

[1] Sir J. Stephens, Lectures on the Hist. of France. Lect. xxiv, p. 710.

[2] Prof. E. Robertson, Art. on Law, Enc. Brit. ed. 1882, "Sir Henry
Maine has associated its rise with the activity of modern legislatures,
which is, of course, *a characteristic of the societies in which English laws
prevail.*"

[3] Sir Henry Maine, Early Hist. of Institutions, p. 21. "The Roman
Law introduced or immensely stimulated the habit of legislation, and
this is one of the ways in which it has influenced the stubborn body
of Germanic customs prevailing in Great Baitain."

the commons, the lords and the king have all had limits set to their authority by the common law.

France has had no one law acting as the interpreter of a national spirit. "It has been smitten with the curse of an anomalous and dissonant jurisprudence beyond every other country in Europe." [1] Before 1789 it was divided into two great divisions; the provinces in which the *Droit E crit*, or Written Law prevailed, and those in which the *Droit Coutumier* or Customary Law, pravailed. The former, as the basis of their jurisprudence, accepted the written Roman law; the latter only admitted it in so far as it was conformable to their local usages, and then it mainly supplied judicial expressions and forms of legal reasoning. There was still further division. Where the Customary Law was in force, each commune, city,[2] and province[3] had its own customs, and where the Written Law was observed, the feudal usages that formed a part of it were of a miscellaneous and arbitrary nature.[4] The different customs and usages tended to a disintegration of national thought; each man had more interest in his village or province than in the nation. The arbitrary maxims of Rome made the law itself subservient to the absolute power of the crown. It needed the French Revolution to wipe out this anonalous mass of jurisprudence, and to furnish one law

---

[1] Sir Henry Maine, Ancient Law, p. 80.

[2] Am. Law Rev. vol. xii, p. 262, Parliaments in France. "A man's rights, his responsibilities, and his mode of enforcing them, might vary as he passed from one village to another. He could breakfast at Nismes without fear of the terrors of the law, only to find himself when he reached Arles subject to its direct penalties.

[3] Kitchin's Hist. of France, vol. ii, p. 457. "In the reign of Henry IV, Dauphiny struggled hard to get the tax shifted from personal to real property, a boon so needful for a poor and hilly country. Languedoc, her wealthy neighbor, was actually under the other system, and had her taxation based on real property."

[4] De Tocqueville, The Old Regime and the Revolution; Appendix, note on Feudal Rights.

Hallam, H., The Middle Ages, vol. i, chap. 2, part ii.

for every Frenchman and every locality. Certainly, the law administered in the courts of France before 1789 was not fitted to
make the great chartered corporations of justice, so much the
guardians of the liberties of a nation, as the protectors of the
privileges of a province, and of the prerogatives of a king.

Another consequence follows from the difference in law.
Guizot lays down as a primary truth, that[1] "the true principle

Division of
Power.

of representive government is the radical illegitimacy
of all absolute powor, whatever may be its name or
place; that absolute power as a right inheres in none of the
powers, which concur to form the government." Therefore, the
first great external characteristic of representative government is
division of powers

In England for more than a thousand years the law has
always interposed to prevent the encroachment of one order of
the State upon another, and to vindicate the rights of all.
Although the king has at times asserted, he has never established
the claim to inscribe among the laws of the land, edicts issued
upon the sole authority of his prerogative, and no king, since the
time of earliest king-making, has sat upon the throne, without
the recognition of his title, either by his Council of Barons, or
later, his Parliament. The sovereignty of the king has always
been limited,[2] and the power of the government has been shared
among the different orders of the State, in other words, the law
has defined with a degree of clearness the functions and the
limits of the legislative, judicial and executive division of
government.

In France we find no such division resulting from the feudal
and Roman law. The feudal lord combined in himself the
legislative, judicial and executive government of his domain.
Public opinion exercised slight control over him, and his vassal

[1] Guizot, Essays upon Representative Gov. in England. Lect. 1.
[2] Hallam, H., Constitutional Hist. of England, vol. i, chap. 1.

had no right, which it was dangerous for him to disrespect. These two sentences sum up the three contraries to the characteristics of representative government, as Guizot defines them.[1] The Roman law held that every ordinance pronounced in the King's Court was binding throughout his kingdom, thus making the king a legislator; and it furnished the doctrine familiar to every student of modern history, that, " the sovereign is the fountain of all justice," thus making him a judge.

These were the features of the law with which the Parliament of Paris was profoundly familiar, to whose study and practice the counselors had devoted their lives, and by which their habits of thought were determined. No evolution from such an institution could produce the deliberative body of a representative government.

There were certain minor features, peculiar to the French judicial system, that furnish a further answer to the question of Parliamentary development. The sale and hereditary tenure of judicial offices; the privileges of the magistrates, and their exemptions from taxation; the multiplication and dispersion of the Parliaments, which prevented them from acting with the unity of a single body; these facts were real agencies that removed the Parliaments from the sympathies of the people, and did away with the idea of representative connection between them.

Certain minor reasons.

In truth, the Old Régime and the Parliaments were indissolubly bound together; the weakness and the strength of both inhered in the common foundation of kingly absolutism. The opening of the States-General, May 5, 1789, that was the portent of the destruction of old-time royalty, was likewise the presage of the dissolution of the Parliaments of France.

---

[1] Guizot, Essays upon Representative Government in England. Lect. 1. "The three external characteristics of the principle of representative government, are: 1. division of powers; 2. election of officers; 3. publicity of discussion.

www.ingramcontent.com/pod-product-compliance
Lightning Source LLC
Chambersburg PA
CBHW021644270326
41931CB00008B/1155